AF430223

Hello, my name is Kindall, and I am Autistic. That means I see, hear and experience the world differently than other people do.

I start my day with a big smile. I enjoy a yummy bagel with cream cheese for breakfast. After eating, I brush my teeth and get ready for school.

I ride a special van with five other kids to school. The van is small and quiet, which makes me feel comfortable.

It may take me longer to learn things, and that's ok, because I learn differently than you do. Some things I am great at, because, just like you, I am talented too.

At school, I learn in a special classroom with friends and two kind teachers. I enjoy the support and the quiet environment.
3 - 2 =
1 + 1 =
5   4
1

After school I love to have some popcorn and play Roblox on the VR in my room because I am super awesome at video games.

I enjoy playing outside or going to the park with my mom and my dad, the swing is my favorite because I feel like I am flying.

I am very cautious, which may cause me to get nervous when someone comes too close to the special space that surrounds me; mom calls it "My Bubble." That is because I do not understand what is happening or how to react.

Sometimes I feel better when I play by myself, especially when I am doing my artwork
Other times I may feel sad, especially when I am confused about what is going on.
But no matter how I feel, I know it's okay to express my emotions.

I do get curious sometimes to step outside my bubble, but I must do it at my own pace. When I don't understand or get scared,

I may have a "Meltdown." When this happens, you may see me pacing, covering my eyes or rocking back and forth.

Like you, I
have dreams and
goals that i want to
come true. Like being
an artist, being a
scientist or buliding
things. I know with
hard work I can make
my dreams come true.

Sometimes, you may see me cover my ears when there is a lot of noise or when I hear certain sounds, it is because certain things sound different to me than it may sound to you, which makes nervous.

Autism is different for other children who are like me, we are not all the same,
and each moment affects us in different ways. So please be patient and understanding with all of us.

Don't worry, I will get through it with the love and support from others like my mom and my dad.

If you have a friend with autism, be patient and kind. Sometimes, they might need a little extra help or understanding. Being a good friend means being there for each other no matter what.

My family are always there for me, whether I'm feeling happy or sad. We laugh together, play together, and support each other through everything. With them by my side, I know I can do anything.

Sometimes I like to play with my friends when I feel comfortable.

And sometimes I like to sit and watch my friends play until I feel it's okay to join in

I may seem a little strange sometimes because of the way I do things, and that is ok because my mom says that is what makes me special.

It takes me a moment to feel comfortable to play with others, so please be patient I just have to take my time.

Once I get to know my friends I enjoy doing things with them, like going to the zoo or other cool places

If we take the time to learn and understand each other than that is how friendships are made, and we can feel welcomed to have fun with each other

Someone with autism may look like you and I, we just may do things differently than most kids, because it is how we see the world but our differences is what makes us unique, just like a puzzle piece,

Being different is what makes us special!
Just like some people love to draw, and
others love to dance, everyone has their
own superpowers. We're all awesome in our
own way!

We can learn more about autism by reading books or talking to grown-ups. Learning helps us understand each other better and be even better friends!
AUTISM

Being a friend to me means to be understanding, kind, helpful and sticking up for one another, in times when your friend can't stick up for themselves.

Even little actions can make a big difference! Whether it's sharing toys or helping out in the community, we can all do our part to make the world a better place for everyone.

No matter who you are or where you come
from, everyone deserves to be treated with
kindness and respect. By embracing our
differences and celebrating what makes
us unique, we can create a world where
everyone feels accepted and valued.

Despite the challenges I may face, I never give up hope, and for me my friends, family and the love that surrounds me gives me the strength to keep trying because I know they are there for me every step of the way.

A- is for "Autism" and Autism is me.

U- is for "Unique" when it comes to me you see.

T- is for "Tough", so I will keep trying every day.

I- is for "Inspirational" as I shine in all my glory.

S- is for "Special" as I grow and share my story.

M- is for the "Memories" that we will share along the way.

www.ingramcontent.com/pod-product-compliance
Lightning Source LLC
Chambersburg PA
CBHW040207160726

48006CB00014B/1927